# I Am Tyrannosaurus Rex

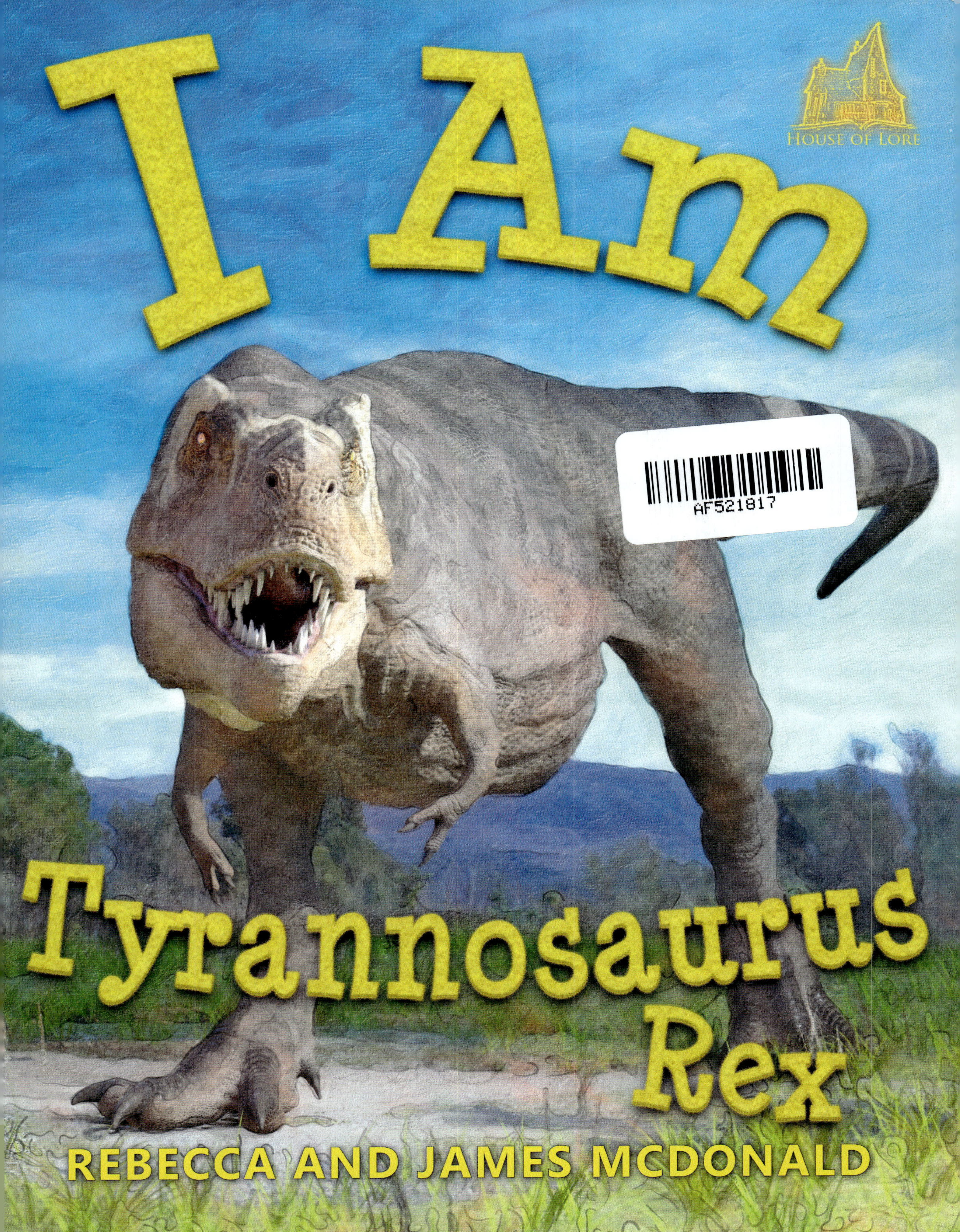



REBECCA AND JAMES MCDONALD

I am Tyrannosaurus rex. Millions of years ago, I roamed the Earth, searching for food. I'm one of the biggest meat-eating dinosaurs that ever lived.

My name Tyrannosaurus rex means tyrant lizard king, but my nickname is T-Rex.

Scientists call dinosaurs like me, that stand on two legs and eat meat, theropods.

Walking on two legs is easy with my long and thick tail. It helps me keep my balance and run fast, so I can catch other dinosaurs.

Just because I'm really big and have a mouth full of super sharp teeth, doesn't mean catching dinner is easy. Some dinosaurs are fast and manage to get away.

Other dinosaurs have clever ways of escaping, like running in large groups that confuse me, or hiding in water.

Some dinosaurs with spiked or clubbed tails are really good at defending themselves.

When food gets scarce, I have to watch out for other Tyrannosaurus rex who might try to make a meal of me!

As big as I am, I still have to be on the lookout for even bigger dinosaurs. If a bigger dinosaur tries to eat me, I run!

And if there's no chance to run, I stay and fight.

When I was a baby, I started out in an egg. Scientists have found dinosaur nests with several eggs, so I probably have sisters and brothers.

The eggs that have been found are a lot smaller than the dinosaurs who laid them, so it wasn't easy for dinosaur parents to keep their eggs safe from being crushed or eaten.

Scientists believe some dinosaur eggs were speckled, so they would blend in with the surroundings and be easier to hide. Other dinosaurs buried their eggs in soft sand and would dig them up later when the eggs were ready to hatch.

A fully grown Tyrannosaurus rex doesn’t have to worry so much about being hunted, but when I was a baby there were all kinds of dangers to look out for.

My parents taught me how to hunt and take care of myself, but they could only look after me for so long. In order to survive, I had to be good at hiding and staying out of trouble.

I was growing fast, so finding as much food to eat as I could without becoming a snack for bigger dinosaurs was really important. Luckily, I have sharp eyesight and a sensitive nose.

Some scientists believe that I have scaly skin like a lizard or snake.

Other scientists think that I have feathers.

Whether covered with scales or feathers, many scientists agree that theropods slowly changed over time into the birds that you see today.

I no longer walk the Earth, but as people find more Tyrannosaurus rex bones, they will understand more of the story of how I lived my life.

What do you think the skin of a Tyrannosaurus rex looked like?

Can you name some things that dinosaurs have in common with birds?

What do you think a Tyrannosaurus rex nest looked like?

Why do you think some dinosaurs arranged their eggs in a circle when nesting?

I Am Tyrannosaurus Rex



ISBN: 978-1-950553-00-6
First House of Lore paperback edition, 2019
Visit us at www.HouseOfLore.net

I Am Earth
Rebecca and James McDonald
I Am the Solar System
REBECCA AND JAMES MCDONALD
I Am the Moon
REBECCA AND JAMES MCDONALD
I Am the Sun
REBECCA AND JAMES MCDONALD
I Am A Bee
I Am Spring
I Am A Dinosaur
I Am Triceratops
CHECK OUT THESE OTHER TITLES FROM HOUSE OF LORE
Bo the Bear BUILDS a Monster Truck
REBECCA AND JAMES MCDONALD
Bo the Bear BUILDS a Race Car
REBECCA AND JAMES MCDONALD
Why Mama Why
Rainy Day Poems
The Scribbles
REBECCA AND JAMES MCDONALD
Through The Milky Way On A PB&J
James McDonald
Wilford and Blue
The Kite Calamity
REBECCA AND JAMES MCDONALD
Petey And The Bee
A Dog's Tale
Do I Look Odd To You
Rebecca and James McDonald
Rebecca and James McDonald
James McDonald

Made in the USA
Las Vegas, NV
03 February 2021

17132531R00029